PROCESS THEOLOGY AND PASTORAL CARE

BRUCE G. EPPERLY

Topical Line Drives
Volume 33

Energion Publications
Gonzalez, Florida
2019

ISBN10: 1-63199-644-4
ISBN13: 978-1-63199-644-3

Energion Publications
P. O. Box 841
Gonzalez, FL 32560

energion.com
pubs@energion.com

TABLE OF CONTENTS

CHAPTER ONE

THE SPIRIT OF PROCESS THEOLOGY

One night, a weary pilgrim dreamed that he saw a ladder, upon which angels were ascending from earth to heaven and then back again. He received a promise of a glorious future and blessings beyond belief, and then awakened with fear and trembling, stammering "surely God is in this place and I did not know it." Upon further reflection, the pilgrim asserted, "How awesome is this place! This is none other than the house of God, and this is the gate of heaven." (Genesis 28:16–17)

Years later, this same pilgrim was confronted by a divine being, with whom he wrestled from sundown to daybreak. Although his opponent had the upper hand in size and endurance, the pilgrim would not let go, and demanded, "I will not let you go unless you bless me." At daybreak, the pilgrim is blessed by his nocturnal combatant, and given a new name. Once Jacob, now he is Israel, "for you have striven with God and human beings, and have prevailed" (Genesis 32:26, 28). Once again, the pilgrim proclaims God's nearness, "I have seen God face to face and my life is spared" (Genesis 32:30).

In Jacob's nocturnal adventures, we glimpse the outlines of the church's pastoral mission in the twenty-first century. Living between earth and heaven, the church's vocation is to awaken persons to the reality of God's presence in the complexities of daily life and civic involvement. There are angels, messengers of God, in our midst that need our attention and response. Pastoral care aims at the affirmation that "God is in this place and now I know it."

Encountering the Living God is not without its challenges and conflicts. Pastoral ministry today is profoundly concrete and incarnational and must wrestle with realities unknown to previous generations — global climate change, religious and cultural pluralism, the decline of institutional authority, the impact of communications and technology, rising racism, new models of parenting and family life, and the growth of psychological aware-ness. Still, amid the radical changes of the past half century, there are constants in human experience to which the church's ministry of pastoral care must respond: the realities of death, aging, and diminishment; the quest for meaning; the need for healing; rela-tionships and sexuality; and the nature of vocation. These eternal and ever-present challenges require us to wrestle not only with our mortality and imperfection, but also with our images of God and humankind. As in previous centuries, Christian leaders and con-gregations are challenged to articulate insightful and inspirational theological visions and spiritual practices to enable persons to nav-igate the wondrously diverse and perilous landscape of our time. Our visions of God and the world shape our mission and response to the world in which we live. Healthy and transformative pastoral care reflects our understandings of God, the world, human nature, suffering, grief, death, social involvement, ethical decision-making, and ultimately hope in ways that open us to God's presence in life's most difficult situations, described as life's "unfixables" by Episco-palian spiritual guide Alan Jones.

This text charts the adventures of congregational pastoral care from the profoundly incarnational and relational vision of process theology, grounded in its affirmation that "God is in this place" and that in "wrestling" with God in the concrete realities of life, we experience God's blessing. Theological reflection begins with our vision of God. In the spirit of the biblical tradition, it is impossi-ble to separate our understanding of God from our understanding of history, creation, and humankind. The God of the universe is profoundly personal, relational, and dynamic. The world in its wondrous diversity reflects divine creative wisdom, even when humankind turns away from its divine vocation. We do not need to import God into the hospital room, counseling session, or soup kitchen. God is already here, quietly — and sometimes dramatical-ly — shaping our experience in sighs too deep for words. Despite God's presence in all things, we need creative theological visions to bring God's presence to consciousness in ways that promote personal and community well-being. In the spirit of the creeds of the church, I believe that theology is best taught through the use of dynamic and open-ended affirmations that serve as the lens through which we experience the world.

My own theological frame of reference is process theology, the theological child of philosophers Alfred North Whitehead and Charles Hartshorne, brought to Christian attention by theologians such as John Cobb, David Griffin, Bernard Loomer, and Norman Pittenger, Jay McDaniel, Rita Nakashima Brock, Mary Elizabeth Moore, Philip Clayton, and Catherine Keller. Process theology makes the following affirmations about the universe, human experience, and divinity.

Interdependence. No person is an island. All things are connected and shape one another. Each moment of experience arises from its environment and shapes its response to the world in its own unique way. We are part of an intricate and interdependent tapestry of relationships, beginning with our family of origin and our communities and culture, and embracing the planet as a whole. My well-being is dependent on the health of the environment and my actions ripple across my immediate neighborhood and the community as a whole, adding to or subtracting from the well-being of the whole.

Creativity. Each moment of experience is profoundly shaped by its immediate and distant past. Childhood experiences of joy and trauma and trust and mistrust shape how we experience the world throughout our lives. Yet, we not condemned to repeat the past, even the joyful past. Each moment brings a new creation and the possibility to rise above our past, noticing the impact of trauma and negativity, while choosing new pathways of responsiveness and decision-making. Process theology embodies the apostle Paul's counsel to the Romans: "Do not be conformed to this world, but be transformed by the renewing of your minds, so that you may discern what is the will of God — what is good and acceptable and perfect" (Romans 12:2). Agency is not optional; we are creators and artists of experience, adding something new to the universe with every thought, feeling, or action. Despite the past, we can

5

begin again, we can repent and turn around and become new creations.

Process. The process is the reality, Whitehead asserts. Life is an ever-flowing stream, never standing still, but surging toward the future. Order and innovation, stability and change, are at the heart of reality. In fact, God is the source of novelty, interjecting God's vision of Shalom, of wholeness, to lure the world forward toward new spiritual horizons.

Possibility. Each moment joins past, present, and future. Foundational though it is, the past shapes, but does not determine the future. The limitations of the past — even the most severe limitations brought about by injustice, racism, and oppression — are also the womb of possibility and concrete creativity. In this holy moment, the call of the future lures us forward. The world is unfinished and so are we. God does not have an absolute blue print for the future but encourages new possibilities to emerge as the result of human freedom and creativity, institutional decision-making, environmental influences, and God's own vision of truth, beauty, and goodness. We can live faithfully in the present and hopefully toward the future because:

> *The steadfast love of God never ceases,*
> *God's mercies never come to an end;*
> *they are new every morning;*
> *great is your faithfulness.* (Lamentations 3:22–23, AP)

God is not finished with us or the world. There is no predetermined final destination for our planet our ourselves. We are always persons in the making, choosing our own adventures and in the process of choosing — along with God's own decision-making — incarnating new paths for ourselves and our communities.

Divinity. Process theology's vision of God's relationship to the world and humankind is its most inspirational, insightful, and controversial contribution to modern theological reflection. Though often critiqued for its understanding of divine power as relational rather coercive, process theology reflects the Hebraic and Galilean visions of God as adventurous, personal, and intimate rather than the Neoplatonic understanding of God as timeless, deterministic, and immune from creaturely suffering. Process theology sees God in terms of relationship, creativity, freedom, and possibility. In contrast to Aristotle's "unmoved mover," process theologians see God as the "most moved mover." God is uniquely intimate: we can "take it to the Lord in prayer," because God "knows our every weakness." God is, according to Whitehead, the fellow sufferer who understands. God is also the joyful companion who celebrates our moments of healing, inspiration, and achievement. The Infinite is the most intimate, sharing our history and ongoing evolution of the planet, and out of God's companionship with the world, providing relevant possibilities for creativity, growth, and healing.

God is the inspiration for our adventures. In an unfinished world, God is also in process. God is constantly doing a new thing, urging the world forward toward beauty, reconciliation, and wholeness. The future is open for God and for us, and our creativity, commitment, and courage help shape the future. We are co-creators and companions with God, not passive instruments of divine predestination. Divine providence is constantly at work in the world, providing us with visions and possibilities and the energy to achieve them, but even God's providential guidance awaits our decisions. Like a good and faithful parent, God rejoices in our creativity and agency. Not locked in a timeless vision, God adventures along with us, taking on the risk of human freedom and creativity and the uncertainty of the future. God aims us toward Shalom, wholeness of body, mind, spirit, and community, but God cannot ensure any particular outcome in advance. Still, God's faithfulness is enduring and God's mercies are new every morning and sufficient to inspire us to embody God's vision on earth as it is in heaven. "God is the poet of the world, with tender patience leading it by his vision of truth, beauty, and goodness."[1]

Life-transforming pastoral care reflects the holistic vision of process theology. It is dynamic, relational, holistic, interdisciplinary, adventurous, and open-ended. It embraces the whole person

1 Alfred North Whitehead, *Process and Reality: Corrected Edition (New York: Free Press)*, 346.

in her or his community and seeks to create communities of care, committed to create something beautiful for God as God's companions in healing the world.

CHAPTER TWO
THE PRIESTHOOD OF COMPANIONS

When I lived in Washington DC, I regularly walked by a church marquee that announced, "Where all are pilgrims and none are strangers." I adopted this affirmation in my pastoral work at an historic congregational church on Cape Cod, Massachusetts. These words reflect the essence of process theology and the spirit of Christian community at its best, the dynamic and interdependent nature of life, in which despite our differences we are connected. The church's vocation is to become a place where all are pilgrims and none are strangers, breaking down the walls and healing the wounds of economic disparity, race and ethnicity, gender and sexual diversity, political polarization, addiction and mental health, and human ability.

We are all "pilgrims." We are all on journey in which the process is the reality. We are all growing in wisdom, stature, and awareness of God. No has arrived. No one is finished. There is no final destination in which we can claim to have complete truth in contrast to our neighbor's falsehood. As Paul asserts in the famous love chapter from 1 Corinthians, "we see in a mirror, dimly." Despite our commitment to our religious tradition and congregational gifts, the treasures of our faith are "earthen vessels," imperfect and finite in nature (1 Corinthians 13:12, 2 Corinthians 4:7). Even Jesus grew in "wisdom and stature" (Luke 2:52). The incompleteness and imperfection of our lives is the source of adventure, humility, and companionship on life's journey. A pilgrim faith is constantly open to new understandings of God's revelations within human experience and is willing to seek truth and wholeness wherever it may be found, including the opinions of those with whom we differ and people outside the church.

No one is a "stranger." We are all connected in an intricate web of relationships in which, consciously or unconsciously, we are constantly shaping each other's experience. The wisdom of Zimbabwe and South Africa describes "ubuntu" — I am because of you — which is the essence of human relatedness. Everyone has a place in Christ's community. No one is left out or forgotten. In fact, Christ comes to us in our interactions with every person, including the companion animals with whom we live. There is no "other." There is no person unrelated to us or bereft of God's love and inspiration. Like the rough-hewn geode, every person possesses a hidden beauty, often unseen by her or his companions. God speaks to us in those experiencing homelessness and poverty, opioid addiction, and mental illness. In every situation, we may be entertaining angels, messengers of God, awaiting our acknowledgement, affirmation, and affection. God touches everyone from the inside and each stranger may be a mirror of divinity calling us to higher purpose.

The apostle Paul spoke of the interdependence of Christian community — and, I believe, life in all its wondrous diversity — in terms of the "body of Christ." God is incarnate in the church and also in the world beyond its walls.

> *Now there are varieties of gifts, but the same Spirit; and there are varieties of services, but the same Lord; and there are varieties of activities, but it is the same God who activates all of them in everyone. To each is given the manifestation of the Spirit for the common good. To one is given through the Spirit the utterance of wisdom, and to another the utterance of knowledge according to the same Spirit, to another faith by the same Spirit, to another gifts of healing by the one Spirit, to another the working of miracles, to another prophecy, to another the discernment of spirits, to another various kinds of tongues, to another the interpretation of tongues. All these are activated by one and the same Spirit, who allots to each one individually just as the Spirit chooses. For just as the body is one and has many members, and all the members of the body, though many, are one body, so it is with Christ. For in the one Spirit we were all baptized into one body—Jews or Greeks, slaves or free—and we were all made to drink of one Spirit. Indeed, the body does not consist of one member but of many... If one member suffers, all suffer together with it; if one member is honored, all rejoice together with it.* (1 Corinthians 12:4–13, 26)

Long before Martin Luther spoke of the "priesthood of all believers," the apostle Paul made several process-relational affirmations in 1 Corinthians 12 about the church's deepest reality:

- The church is a dynamically interdependent community.
- Everyone in the church, regardless of age, intellectual or physical ability, or life experience, is inspired by God and has a gift for service.
- God nurtures our various and unique gifts in the course of our lifetime for the good the community and the world.
- Unity and diversity complement each other: we are one preciously because we are each unique, and our uniqueness springs from the unity of God's Spirit moving within our lives and communities.
- The health of the community depends on the well-being of each part. No one's joy or pain is separate from my own.
- The goal of "life together," to quote German theologian Dietrich Bonhoeffer, is growth in wisdom and stature through which I identify my achievements and well-being with the achievements and well-being of my neighbor.
- Everyone is honored, embraced, welcomed, and supported within Christian community.
- Spiritual growth involves recognizing my own gifts at each season of life and supporting the gifts of my fellow pilgrims in Christ.
- The humblest members can be the source of my wholeness and salvation.
- The community's health comes from its commitment to embrace and support the gifts of the persons in the surrounding culture, welcoming them to share in God's holy adventure in the church and the world.

I read the apostle Paul through the lens of process theology and believe that Paul saw the body of Christ as a living organism that dynamically balanced and connected individuality and community. Paul believed that God's Spirit is ubiquitous within the body of Christ in the same way that scientists are discovering that mind and body can't be separated in human experience. Our thoughts and attitudes shape our overall health, even at a cellular level, and our cellular health influences the well-being of the organism as a whole. Within the world and the church, God is the loving companion and spirit — the guide, inspirer, and challenger — within whom "we live and move and have our being" (Acts 17:28). When we discover that we — personally and as a community — are the "light the world" and then "let our light shine," we glow and become light-givers to pilgrims seeking meaning and wholeness.

In the small town Baptist church of my childhood, we celebrated a simple communion service of grape juice and crackers on the first Sunday of each month. As communion ended, my father, who was the congregation's pastor, announced "and when they sang a hymn they went out." Then we sang John Fawcett's "Blest Be the Tie that Binds."

> Blest be the tie that binds
> Our hearts in Christian love;
> The fellowship of kindred minds
> Is like to that above.
>
> Before our Father's throne,
> We pour our ardent prayers;
> Our fears, our hopes, our aims are one,
> Our comforts, and our cares.
>
> We share our mutual woes,
> Our mutual burdens bear;
> And often for each other flows
> The sympathizing tear.

This childhood hymn reflects pastoral theology at its best. What we believe shapes our practices within the community of faith and in the world beyond the church. Within the body of Christ, we are one in God's Spirit and each one us can minister to our brothers and sisters in Christ. The body of Christ, first, is a *community of care and compassion* in which everyone has a role as a companion and healer. While pastor has a special responsibility as spiritual leader of the congregation, everyone has a pastoral vocation to enrich the body of Christ by sharing her or his gifts in ways that serve the larger community and the world. God is at work not just in the pastor's ministry but in the ministry of the whole church, moment by moment and encounter by encounter. The body of Christ is also a *community of listening and affirmation.* A North African desert father spoke of the monk as being "all eye." Within Christ's community, we aspire to be "all sense" as we listen for the divinity emerging in one another. As feminist theologian Nelle Morton counseled, we hear each other into speech, whether our companion is a three year old racing up the aisle for the children's sermon, a teen discerning her or his sexual identity, a young adult seeking a vocational path with a heart, a retiree in search of generativity in the next season of life, or an elder coming to terms with her or his mortality and diminishment. In hearing one another, we become companions in their own growing self-awareness and discovery of God's visions for their lives. Our hearing ourselves in hearing one another becomes an affirmation that "God is in your life — and now you know it!"

The body of Christ is a *community of prayer and action.* Spirituality belongs to the whole people of God. Clergy and laity alike are inspired by God's vision of truth, beauty, and goodness and challenged to do something beautiful for God. Pastoral ministry begins with prayerful practices that eventuate in acts of kindness, healing, and reconciliation. Our whole persons, body and spirit can be a prayer. As Rabbi Abraham Joshua Heschel noted after marching with Martin Luther King, "I felt as if my legs were praying."

The process-relational vision of the body of Christ invites each congregation to become a *community of learning and social concern.* At best, faithful learning is holistic in nature, embracing mind, body, and spirit and individual growth and social transformation. In prayerful learning, we grow both in our understanding of God and our understanding of the world. We embark on spiritual adventures in which we discover the transformative gifts of theologians and spiritual guides but also the unexpected, but transformative, gifts of persons experiencing homelessness and addiction as well as persons from other faiths, cultures, and sexual expressions. In experiencing the holiness of the "other," we realize that as we serve, we grow in wisdom, stature, and insight. In a community of prayerful concern, everyone can become our teacher and spiritual guide.

Luther captured the spirit of Christian community when he asserted that Christians are called to be little Christs, mediating God's grace to one another. Christ is already here in this place and the person with whom we interact. Our vocation, wherever we are in Christian community, is to be midwives of divinity, assisting God in bringing forth the beauty and love waiting to be born in our companions in faith and beyond the walls of the church. As we will discover in the next chapter, this involves claiming our calling to be God's companions in healing the world in interpersonal relationships, congregational care, and social transformation.

CHAPTER THREE
A COMMUNITY OF HEALERS

Jesus was a healer and the church is called to be a community of healers, praying and acting to transform bodies, minds, spirits, relationships, social and political practices, and the planet so that all creation may reflect God's vision of truth, beauty, and goodness. As we ponder the healing vocation of the church — in many ways, the heart of pastoral care — we claim Jesus' mission statements as our own spiritual GPS and personal and congregational inspiration. The church is called to be the body of Christ, reflecting and embodying the way of Jesus in its care for one another within the church and its commitment to healing the world.

> "The Spirit of the Lord is upon me,
> because he has anointed me
> to bring good news to the poor.
> He has sent me to proclaim release to the captives
> and recovery of sight to the blind,
> to let the oppressed go free,
> to proclaim the year of the Lord's favor." (Luke 4:18–19)
>
> I came that they might have life and have it abundantly.
> (John 10:10)

From a process perspective, the quest for healing is holistic, relational, and universal. Pastoral care is both individual and social in focus. In the spirit of pastoral theologian Henri Nouwen, the church's vocation is to be a community of "wounded healers," aware of our own brokenness and sin and open to the unconditional healing love of God. Though wounded, every Christian is called to share in Jesus' healing ministry in the journey toward becoming a "healed healer," mediating God's grace to suffering humanity. Our joys and sorrows are one, and the healing of others contributes to our own wholeness. Our personal well-being is connected to the well-being of our families, communities, nation, and the planet.

In the body of Christ, incarnate in our own psycho-physical-spiritual lives and in the communities to which we belong, everything is connected. In the human body, the health of a group of cells shapes a well-being for good or ill. The same applies to a congregation or community. The quality of life of one sector in society contributes to the health or disease of the social order.

Pastoral care addresses our spiritual and emotional issues. But, its context is always relational, social, and political. Our society's attitudes toward race, sexuality, immigration, and economics, shape the quality of life not only of the vulnerable but also, as the prophet Amos notes, the spiritual and emotional lives of the privileged and wealthy, often complicit with or responsible for systems that diminish the lives of the poor, vulnerable, marginalized, and outsider. Compare these words of Amos 8:11–12, addressed to the avaricious and apathetic upper class, with Jesus mission statement from Luke 4:18–19, described earlier in this chapter:

> *The time is surely coming, says the Lord GOD,*
> *when I will send a famine on the land;*
> *not a famine of bread, or a thirst for water,*
> *but of hearing the words of the Lord.*
> *They shall wander from sea to sea,*
> *and from north to east;*
> *they shall run to and fro, seeking the word of the Lord,*
> *but they shall not find it.*

Process theology inspires a vision of pastoral care that joins personal health with social justice, political access, and planetary care. Over a century ago, social gospel leader Walter Rauschenbusch asserted "Hell's Kitchen [once the home of impoverished immigrants] is not a safe place for saved souls." Today, we know that our personal health is shaped by our working conditions, economic status, education, political access, and environment as well as our prayers, diet, spiritual practices, exercise, and lifestyle choices. Relationship is everything, whether we speak of our children's hopes and dreams or our recovery from serious illness. In the spirit of Jesus, the church is called to be a community of healing prayer and prophetic care.

Pastoral Care and Healing Prayer. Every Sunday at the church I pastor, we have a time of community prayer, integrating prayers of gratitude and joy with prayers of intercession, petition, and concern. The prayers of concern range from issues related to physical well-being (most especially, cancer and chronic illness) to addiction and global concerns. We pray for peace of mind and peace on earth, for wisdom in our personal lives and among the leaders of our nation and the world. Our prayers are cries for help and expressions of our solidarity with those who suffer; they are also calls for God's blessing in relationship to issues beyond our control. Our prayers assume that the God hears our prayers and seeks our well-being and that the future is open and can be altered in the intimate interdependence of human aspiration and divine compassion.

Our prayers are grounded in God's creative-responsive love. God is, as the parent of process theology Alfred North Whitehead asserts, the fellow sufferer who understands. God is also the intimate companion who seeks abundant life for all creation and each person. Prayer changes us, and it also changes God's experience of the world. In an interdependent universe, our prayers are not limited by space or time, but create a field of force around those for whom we pray, subtly changing their lives and creating an environment which enables God's intimate vision to be more fully embodied in our lives and the subjects of our prayers.

Pastoral care is prayerful concern in the spirit of Jesus' ministry of healing, reconciliation, and transformation. Pastoral care aims at healing and wholeness of body, mind, and spirit, whether in personal conversation, hospital and home visitation, community worship, and liturgical healing services. In the body of Christ, we reach out to one another as embodiments of Jesus' healing ministry. Jesus' ministry transformed cells as well as souls and created a world in which the marginalized and vulnerable find themselves at the center of God's concern. The first Christian communities were dynamic pilgrim communities in which no one was a stranger or outsider, but everyone part of God's coming realm of Shalom.

Today's healing arts involve the integration of high tech and high touch. While most persons seeking healing today are receiving medical care, process theologians also recognize that whole person healing requires chemotherapy and conversation, prayer and Prozac, medication and medication, and physical therapy and friendly faces. Medical studies not only suggest that prayer be a factor in recovery from surgery but that involvement in congregational life and service to the community is a factor in longevity, stress reduction, recovery from illness, and healthy relationships. No one can overestimate the power of prayer and loving conversation to transform our lives. Accordingly, the first movement of congregational pastoral care is prayerful communion that takes us beyond individualism to love others as we love ourselves.

Prayerful communion invites pastoral caregivers to embrace a wide variety healing arts from psychotherapy to energy work. Our congregation is one of many throughout North America to hold reiki, and other healing touch clinics. Welcome and loving touch is essential to well-being, whether it involves liturgical healing services and the laying on of hands, energy work, hugs, and passing the peace. Of course, it goes without saying that healing touch is always aimed the other's best interests and is conducted with the highest ethical standards and clear boundaries. The focus of healing touch is the well-being of the one receiving treatment and not our own pleasure or domination. Our goal in every aspect of the congregation's ministry, and most especially in healing touch, is to do something beautiful for God and loving for our brothers and sisters.[2]

Pastoral Care as Open-heartedness. Mystic Etty Hillesum, who died during the Holocaust, once confessed that her aspiration was to be a "thinking heart," intellectually astute and emotionally present to others. In similar fashion, process theologian Bernard

---

2 For more on ministries of healing and wholeness, see Bruce Epperly, *The Energy of Love: Reiki and Christian Healing* (Gonzalez, FL: Energion, 2017); *Healing Marks: Healing and Spirituality in Mark's Gospel* (Gonzalez, FL: Energion, 2012); *Reiki Healing Touch and the Way of Jesus* (Kelowna, BC: Northstone, 2005); and *God's Touch: Faith, Wholeness, and the Healing Miracles of Jesus* (Louisville: Westminster/John Knox, 2001).

Loomer, with whom I studied at Claremont Graduate School, described size or stature as one of the most important spiritual values. Jesus grew in "wisdom and stature" and that is our calling too.

> By size I mean the stature of a person's soul, the range and depth of his love, his capacity for relationships. I mean the volume of life you can take into your being and still maintain your integrity and individuality, the intensity and variety of outlook you can entertain in the unity of your being without feeling defensive or insecure. I mean the strength of your spirit to encourage others to become freer in the development of their diversity and uniqueness.[3]

Pastoral care is grounded in our ability to embrace the experience of another without judgment, condescension, or distaste. For pastors and laypersons alike, this is often challenging, especially when people share their stories of addiction, trauma, violent and abusive behavior, and ethical failure. We often hear stories of victims' violence, abuse, manipulation, infidelity, or unforgiveness. Those who share their lives often fear that we will turn away in judgment and condemnation.

Sadly, many persons condemn those whom they don't understand as a result of their understanding of God. They worship a God who creates walls between the saved and unsaved, faithful and infidel, and moral and reprobate and commands us to do likewise. They see God as the ultimate "hanging judge," out to get us, watching our every move and prepared to chastise us for the least offense against divinely-sanctioned rules and regulations. Their "hate the sin but love the sinner" theologies end up shaming the sinner and worse yet excluding the backslider from eternal life. In contrast, process theology sees God as the Heart of the Universe, who knows our fallibility yet loves us anyway. Indeed, God loves us long before we repent; we are loved because we are God's own, and there is nothing we can do to thwart that love.

Process theology envisions God as the "circle whose center is everywhere and whose circumference is nowhere." No one is

---

3 Bernard Loomer, "S-I-Z-E is the Measure," Harry James Cargas and Bernard Lee, *Religious Experience and Process Theology* (Mahweh, NJ: Paulist Press, 1976), 70.

excluded from God's love or our ministries. Sin and guilt are real, our mistakes can do great harm to others and ourselves and haunt us across decades, yet sin and guilt are calls to healing not condemnation. God is not out to get us; God is out to love us as God presents us in every moment of our lives the opportunity to chart a new path, adapt new behaviors, and forgive and be forgiven.

A God of Loving Stature inspires loving stature in pastoral care givers who listen without judgment and who embrace the breadth of experience with grace and acceptance. Other peoples' experiences may not always be understandable, given our own values and experience, but they can be embraceable as we align our spirits with the Spirit of the fellow sufferer who understands. We can hear each other into speech and love each other into change, healing by listening, and helping people to claim their responsibility without shaming them or creating guilt where none truly exists. Holy listening enables the other to hear God's voice within their pain and guilt and awaken them to God's relentless vision of healing possibilities at every stage of life. "God is the ideal companion who transmutes what has been lost into a living fact within his own nature. He is the mirror that discloses to every creature its own greatness."[4]

Prophetic Acts. Process theology is profoundly relational. Whitehead asserts that the whole universe conspires to create each moment of experience. Accordingly, pastoral care must take into consideration environmental and family issues as essential to the healing process. African American mystic Howard Thurman asserts that one of the greatest evils created by poverty is the stunting of children's imaginations and dreams of the future. The future is the house of hope and the realm of possibility, in which today's limits can give birth to tomorrow's adventures. Poverty, injustice, sexism, racism, and homophobia, not to mention persecution based on religion and citizenship, replace dreams with despair and aspirations with apathy. They stand in the way of God's dream for our children and future generations.

---

4 Alfred North Whitehead, *Religion in the Making* (Cambridge: Cambridge University Press, 2011), 48

Pastoral care must include public health and public policy and be preventative in nature. The church is called to prevent, and not just respond to, emotional distress, mental health issues, and trauma by working toward God's Shalom in the boardroom, public sphere, and domestic life. Family values are grounded in good work, accessible health care, safe communities, and quality education, all of which are profoundly economic and political in nature. Prophetic pastoral care leads to prophetic action that confronts gun violence at its sources and promotes healthy environments, safe and excellent schools, accessible health care, and employment opportunity. It is impossible to ensure completely the mental and physical health of children, youth, and adults if they are surrounded by a culture of greed, inequality, racism, sexism, and violence. These issues may drive congregations from prayer to the picket lines and pastoral care sessions to political involvement. Each congregation will have to assess its own style of political involvement, while recognizing that non-involvement is also a political statement.

God's vision of Shalom transcends political party and the labels of liberal, moderate, or conservative. Still Shalom means a commitment in the household as well as the Houses of Congress to *"let justice flow down like waters and righteousness like an ever-flowing stream"* (Amos 5:24). Healed people create healthy social structures, and healthy social, political, and domestic institutions create the foundations for healthy personal development and family life.

Pastoral Care as Self-care. Process theologians recognize the reality of sin, although they challenge the doctrines of original sin and human depravity. As the creation story from Genesis 1 proclaims, God created the world "good." Though sin is universal, it cannot overcome the "original goodness" of creation and every child. God's light shines in every life, forever and always, regardless of how far he or she has strayed from God's vision. Accordingly, self-care for pastoral care givers is not optional. It is essential to our healthy care for others and the health of our personal and community ministries over the long haul. This is often challenging since many care givers act as if God cares for everyone except themselves and that while others need support, they can go it alone.

Such spiritual individualism often leaves in its wake compassion fatigue, burnout, and boundary violations. In the interdependent and benevolent universe, charted by process theology, God loves each of us fully and unconditionally and wants us to flourish and grow into the image of Jesus. God is constantly working in our lives, inspiring us both to trust God and reach out to others as the foundation of our caring ministries.

Grace inspires us to be graceful and gracefulness begins with our self-affirmation and self-care. We are finite and prone to self-interest that hurts us and others. Self-awareness holds in tension both our beauty and our limitations. We are all, in the spirit of the hymn I learned in my childhood Baptist church, "standin' in the need of prayer." God never abandons us, but in fact is our constant inspiration and guide, even when we struggle to care for others as well as ourselves.

> *Likewise the Spirit helps us in our weakness; for we do not know how to pray as we ought, but that very Spirit intercedes with sighs too deep for words. And God, who searches the heart, knows what is the mind of the Spirit, because the Spirit intercedes for the saints according to the will of God. In all things God works for God, for those who love God and are called according to God's purpose.* (Romans 8:26–28, AP)

God wants us to love our neighbors and God wants us to love ourselves. The world is saved one person at a time and that includes us as well as those whom we serve. Accordingly, the church is a community of health, promoting the well-being of every member, including those who are called to ministries of compassionate pastoral care. Given the realities of compassion fatigue and care giver burnout, every member is invited to explore ways of self-care and spiritual formation, appropriate to her or his life situation and personality type. In addition to outreach ministries and ministry teams such as Stephen Ministries, healthy congregations have courses in prayer, meditation, reiki healing touch and holistic health, responding to stress, physical well-being, and responding to family of origin issues. We all need healing, and God is moment by moment providing us possibilities that bless us so that we can in our pastoral care be blessings to others. In our intentional self-healing, often through counseling and spiritual direction, we claim our role as God's companions in healing the world one person at a time.

CHAPTER FOUR

NURTURING SPIRITUAL RESILIENCE

On the verge of adulthood, Jesus goes with his parents and other pilgrims to the Jerusalem Temple. He is so engrossed in dialogue with the Temple priests that he forgets to join the returning pilgrims. When his parents notice he is missing, they anxiously search for him and when they discover him at the Temple, his mother challenges his thoughtlessness. The future Teacher and Healer deflects their questions with the affirmation that he is taking the first steps in embracing his vocation. The passage ends with the affirmation that Jesus "grew in wisdom and in stature, and in divine and human favor" (Luke 2:52).

Jesus' process of spiritual and emotional differentiation was painful to his parents, but it is necessary for every child to discover her or his passion and vocation in creative interdependence with family and friends. From the very beginning of life, congregational pastoral care seeks to nurture children whose sense of God's presence in their lives enables them to discover where their deep passions meet the needs of the world, as Frederick Buechner reminds us. In every moment of life from conception to death, God is presenting us with creative possibilities, congruent with our life experiences, environment, maturity, and previous decisions. God's vision for us is both moment by moment, for our unique season and context, and for the long haul. God calls and we respond, leading to new divine possibilities in our lives. Pastoral care helps parents and children grow into God's vision for themselves and the well-being of the community and planet.

Over our lifetime, pastoral care and faith formation are intimately connected in the intricate interdependence of life, beginning with the nurture of parenting skills and healthy family life. Briefly put, pastoral care nurtures from the very beginning feelings of trust, security, value, competence, responsibility, self-affirmation, and service. Recognizing that no one escapes the challenges of life, whether, spiritual, relational, physical, or emotional, strength of character — able to withstand the storms of life — is an essential goal of self-actualization and mature faith. Process theology sees the following affirmations as essential to its message for children and the child in all of us:

- God loves you unconditionally.
- God cherishes your uniqueness.
- God wants you to develop your gifts for self-fulfillment and service.
- God is trustworthy in every season of life and calls forth trustworthy adults to be companions, friends, and mentors.
- God has a dream for your life, which emerges in the dynamic call and response of divine possibility and human decision-making.
- You are God's beloved child and you can't lose that love.
- Even when you lose your way, you are still in God's care and God will send resources in the form of persons, situations, and encounters to help you find your way.

As a laboratory for growth and resilience, the church's message life-affirming to children: God loves you, we love you, and you can make a difference!

In this awe-inspiring world, life can still be difficult. Our sense of trust and value may be threatened in the storms of life. At such moments, congregational care givers claim their role as companions and mirrors of God's promise, who believe when we can't believe, who hope when we've lost hope, and love us when we feel most unlovable. As a community of healers, church-sponsored pastoral care during difficult times takes many forms: recovery groups, support groups for parents of children and grandchildren dealing with addiction or mental health issues, bereavement groups for parents and for children. These groups remind us through the witness of others that God is with us, God loves us, God will never give up on us, and that God has a vision for us that will outlast life's traumas and disappointments. As congregations grow in wisdom and stature, they become homes for wayward pilgrims, prayerfully and carefully embracing the angels and demons we all face. In the intricate interdependence of life, we are all in this together, there is no other or outsider. We are all pilgrims, touched by God and consciously or unconsciously seeking to align our lives with God's vision of Shalom. As noted preacher Ernie Campbell once claimed, "there are only two kinds of people in the world — those who are in God's hands and know it and those who are in God's hands and don't."

The quest for resilience takes us beyond our congregation's walls to embrace the social order. No child or adult lives in isolation but is shaped by their social context. Pastoral care within the congregation soon takes us beyond the congregation in the quest for healing structures in the social order. Patterns of violence, neglect, and injustice — whether personal, institutional, or governmental, stunt our spirits and imprison our imaginations. God's vision — and thus the scope of possibility — becomes blurred for victims of violence, racism, trauma, and ostracism. The quest for spiritual resilience inspires us to create — or rehabilitate — structures of self-affirmation, well-being, character, and courage. Advocacy is not optional once we realize the interconnectedness of life. Political and cultural advocacy takes beyond our comfort zones to seek wholeness for the least, lost, and lonely, and to provide spiritual sanctuary for undocumented immigrants, homeless veterans, families in crisis, youth questioning their sexual identity, persons bullied because of appearance, ability, intelligence, religion, or nation of origin.

Such open-hearted care calls upon all the stature that a person or congregation can muster and must find a personal foundation in our own appropriation of the affirmations: we are loved, we are valuable, we matter, and that we can learn spiritual practices to deepen our faith and courage for the long haul. In the storms of life, we like Jesus' followers discover that God is with us and that when we keep our eyes on God's way, we can walk on water! This vision of spiritual resilience is captured in Whitehead's understanding of peace that takes us being self-interest to trust and service:

At the heart of the nature of things, there are always the dream of youth and the harvest of tragedy. The Adventure of the Universe starts with the dream and reaps tragic beauty. This is the secret of the union of Zest with Peace — that the suffering attains is end in a Harmony of Harmonies. The immediate experience of this Final Fact, with its union of Youth and Tragedy, is the sense of Peace. In this way the world receives its persuasion towards such possibilities as are possible for its diverse individual occasions.[5]

5   Alfred North Whitehead, *Adventures of Ideas* (New York: Free Press, 1967), 296.

CHAPTER FIVE

LIFE'S UNFIXABLES: GRIEF, AGING, DEATH

Following a major stroke, my father was confined to a nursing home for the remainder of his life. One day, during a visit from his pastor, my father noted "I'm stuck" and then made a wry face and continued "but it's ok." If we live long enough, we experience life's "unfixables" — aging, diminishment, grief, and death. The processive nature of life was pointed out by a member of a Bible study I lead at South Congregational Church. After reading through the genealogies in Genesis 5, she noted that "regardless of how long the forerunners of the Hebraic people lived, including Methuselah who made it to 969 years, the author states 'and he died.' It doesn't make any difference how long we live, eventually we all must die."

Now that I am a member of the Medicare generation soon to be on Social Security, I am profoundly aware of what Judith Viorst describes as life's "necessary losses" — I have given eulogies at the funerals of both of my parents, I have mourned the loss of my only sibling, two of my best friends have died of cancer, contemporaries post accounts of their dying process on Facebook and I see the forces of diminishment operative in my own life, despite exercise, a reasonably healthy diet, a positive attitude toward aging, and regularly spiritual practices. I am now the elder in my family, the *pater familias* of three generations of Epperlys.

Martin Luther once stated, "in the midst of life, we are surrounded by death" and then retorted, "in the midst of death, we are surrounded by life." Process theology recognizes that the greatest evil in life is the process of perpetual perishing itself — we can never maintain the freshness of our most joyful moments as each moment perishes to give rise to the next. Alfred North Whitehead asserted that the most significant metaphysical and spiritual issue we face could be summarized in the lines from a hymn:

> Abide with me,
> Fast falls the eventide.

The process is the reality and yet we desire something enduring through all of life's changes. We want to balance the affirmation "God's mercies are new every morning" with "great is God's faithfulness." As pastor, I find that issues of loss can lead to crises of faith; they can also inspire courage and compassion, when we discover that God's presence comes to us as "a tender care in which nothing is lost....God saves the world as it passes into the immediacy of his own life. It is the judgment of a tenderness which loses nothing that can be saved. It is also the judgment of a wisdom which uses what in the temporal world is mere wreckage."[6]

Responding to Loss. In his classic *A Grief Observed*, C.S. Lewis observes that bereavement is an essential season in every good marriage as necessary to a good marriage as experiences of falling in love and joining in marriage. Eventually one member of each loving couple must journey to the graveside or memorial serve and learn to live without the presence of their beloved. As physicians and nurses note, grief can be harmful to our health — not only in terms of physical, emotional, and psychological well-being but also in terms of mortality within the first year following the death of a spouse, especially among men. Accordingly, an essential aspect of pastoral care involves the healing of those who grieve, so that, in the spirit of the Beatitudes, those who mourn discover they are blessed.

Dag Hammarskjold once counseled: "For all that has been — thanks / For all that shall be — yes!" Pastoral care for the grieving involves the moving from letting go to thanksgiving and hopefulness.

African wisdom asserts that "it takes a village to raise a child." Process theology believes that it takes a village to respond creatively to any life transition from birth to death. Healthy responses to necessary losses such as grief involve ongoing supportive relationships, characterized by companionship, empathy, mirroring, and hopefulness. Congregational caregivers need to be persons of sufficient spiritual and emotional stature, so that they can embrace the pain of grief, without psychologically shutting down or resorting to superficial spiritual platitudes. We need to be able to weep with those

---

6 Alfred North Whitehead, *Process and Reality,* 346.

who weep and rejoice with those who rejoice, while maintaining our own spiritual GPS and professional boundaries. Caregivers need to nurture the art of listening both to the pain of those who grieve and to God's whispers, often coming to us in "sighs too deep for words" (Romans 8:26).

In my own ministry with those who are bereaved, my goal, first of all, is to be spiritually and emotionally open to their experience. Even if I have only a few minutes to prepare for a visit, I take time for the following spiritual practices: first, I pause for silent and prayerful contemplation, centering myself in God's healing center; second, I ask for God's guidance, praying for the right spirit, right response, and right words; third, because visiting the bereaved often involves driving, I pause again for a few minutes once I arrive at the home or hospital to re-center myself and open to divine guidance, trusting that God is constantly providing me with inspiration. In my meetings with persons experiencing bereavement, I listen with my heart as well as my ears, resisting the temptation to fill the silence with verbiage. No topics are off-limits, no anger or doubt is off-putting, for caregivers who believe that God is present in the Holy Here and Now of bereavement. Both caregiver and bereaved are challenged to recognize that you can't avoid "the valley of the shadow of death" — you must go through it with God is your companion! This is not a matter of religious shibboleths, or false piety, but recognizing that our experiences of grief can become "thin places," where God speaks within the pain and despair of both the bereaved and caregiver. With our defenses down, God may break through in ways that open us to the interplay of tragedy and beauty, and we may discover that "God is in this place" of grief and brokenness. As John Cobb asserts, "the call forward is toward intensified life, heightened consciousness, expanded freedom, more sensitive love, but the way lies through the valley of the shadow of death."[7]

As a pastor, I recognize that after several years at my current congregation, I also experience grief and need comfort at the death of a congregant. I must do my own emotional and spiritual "homework" in private to serve the spiritual needs of the community.

---

7 John Cobb, *God and the World* (Eugene, OR: Wipf and Stock, 2000), 56.

Process theology recognizes the healing power of ritual for pastor and congregant alike. In the dynamic processes of life, rituals such as memorial services and funerals join the experience of perpetual perishing and loss with the affirmation of God's intimacy. They honor a life and promote letting go with an awareness of the faithfulness of God's tender care that nothing be lost. Though the form of God's love is always contextual, flexible, and open to change, process theology affirms that God's love never ends. God never abandons us but constantly presents us with hopeful possibilities congruent with the pain and loss we are feeling.

Individuality, meaning, relationship, and everlasting life are nurtured in rituals as well as relationships. From a process perspective, memorial and funeral services are affirmations of life in the face of death. They proclaim:

- Our particular lives are unique and matter to God and others.
- Love outlasts death.
- Our lives are treasured by God.
- Our lives continue in the memory of a community and God's memory.
- God's love is eternal and will guide us to further adventures.
- The boundary between this life and the next is translucent and transparent. Earth and heaven penetrate one another through the power of pray and loving relationships.

Aging as an Invitation to Stature. Process theologian Bernard Loomer once suggested that the concept of ambiguity should be a primary theme of theological reflection. Every advance has a shadow side. Labor-saving devices have made our daily lives more efficient and easier but they have also led to complications and 24/7 professional availability. Radiation therapy can save lives and nuclear energy can power our technology; radiation can also be used to create a "dirty bomb" and accidents such as the Chernobyl nuclear meltdown can render communities uninhabitable. The same ambiguity applies to the aging process. At sixty-six, I can claim a small portion of the wisdom of the years — I feel more generative and spiritually-centered than I did at twenty; I delight in my grandchildren and have professional skills that come from a lifetime committed to study, reflection and spiritual growth. But, I also recognize that, despite my commitment to spiritual practices, a healthy diet, and daily exercise, I am not as energetic as I was in my teens and have to depend on "better living through chemistry" in some areas of my life. Like many baby boomers, I fear the possibility of memory loss, disability, and irrelevance, and wonder "who will I be if I lose the ability to do the things I love." There is no way we can avoid the aging process apart from death through catastrophic illness, accident, or suicide at the height of our physical and intellectual powers!

Process theology recognizes the change brings both transformation and apprehension. To embrace novelty, we have to let go of the past in all its glory. To rejoice in the present, we have to remember that "this is the day that God has made" (Psalm 118:24). This moment is the intersection of time and eternity, and the opportunity to embrace God's vision of truth, beauty, and goodness. In this moment, we can rejoice in the wonder of life and add to the beauty of the world.

Process theology proclaims that God is intimately connected with every moment of life from conception to death, and beyond. Process theology also encourages creativity and agency in every season of life. We are not the passive victims of the aging process; we are artists of our experience who can be generative despite diminishment. We can also activity promote our well-being through healthy lifestyle, spiritual practices, positive relationships, and meaningful activities. The ambiguity of aging can give birth to greater wisdom and generativity. Trusting God's faithful companionship and opening to emerging spiritual possibilities, we can with the Apostle Paul affirm, "we do not lose heart. Even though our outer nature is wasting away, our inner nature is being renewed day by day" (2 Corinthians 4:16). In the context of aging, the church's pastoral care vocation involves providing positive visions of generativity and opportunities for service throughout the aging process

Pastoral care during the aging process focuses on nurturing meaning, vocation, community, and generativity, and can be articulated in terms of the following affirmations that guide the caring process:

- Every moment is an opportunity to experience divine wisdom and love.
- Each person has gifts that contribute to their own joy and the health of those around them, including their congregation.
- Every person is God's beloved and every condition of life is a call to care.
- God is constantly providing us with new possibilities and the appropriate energy to realize them.
- Despite the impact of the aging process, we have the freedom to embark on new adventures in body, mind, and spirit.
- God is our closest companion in health and illness, and joy and sorrow.
- God has a vision for our future and we can glimpse God's vision through spiritual practices and healthy relationships.
- In the interdependence of life, we can open to the gifts and support of others and in receiving their support add zest to their lives.

Pastoral care from a process perspective is ultimately grounded in hopeful relatedness that reminds us that every moment of life can be vocational. Roman Catholic spiritual leader and political activist Dorothy Day spoke out for justice till the day she died and was arrested for non-violent resistance in her mid-seventies. When she was sidelined by serious illness in her late seventies and had to give up managing the *Catholic Worker*, Day confessed that "my job now is prayer." In her creative embrace of diminishment, Day models a spirituality of aging. Physical limitations challenge our sense of meaning, vocation, and identity, and yet they can open up new vista of spirituality. We can transform the world even if we are homebound. What would happen if millions of persons confined to their homes or assisted living or care facilities took an hour each day to pray for embodiment of God's vision of truth, beauty, goodness, and justice for their families, congregations, and the world? I believe that their prayers would create a vast field of force that transform the hearts and minds of nations and their political leaders. Their prayers would create a field of force enabling God's vision of Shalom to be born on "earth as it is in heaven." As the saying goes, "aging is not for the weak," but aging can bring the gifts of prayer, purpose, courage, and creativity for those who are nurtured by caring communities and open their spirits to God's every present vision of creative transformation.

In the Midst of Death, Life. One afternoon, a servant came to his master begging him to lend him his fastest horse. The master responded, "Why do you need such a horse?" To which his servant replied, "I must go to Samarra. I just saw Death in the marketplace and he made a threatening gesture." Being a generous man, the master lent the horse. Being a brazen man, he sought out Death in the marketplace, and queried, "Why did you frighten my servant?" Death replied, "I did not intend to frighten him. I was surprised to see him here in Baghdad. I have an appointment with him tonight on the road to Samarra!" Regardless of our machinations, death is inevitable and unfixable, source of paralyzing fear and invitation to cherish each moment.

The solidarity of life reminds us that we are the dying caring for the dying. Pastoral care is grounded in the recognition of our common mortality and our quest to find meaning in a world where death can strike unexpectedly. Ivan Ilych, in Tolstoy's classic novella, asks "Who will I be when I am no more?" The reality of death, more than any other reality, compels pastoral caregivers and congregations to confront our fears and hopes. Psalm 90:12 asks God to "teach us to count our days that we may gain a wise heart." Denial cannot save us from the inevitable. In facing death in all its finality, trusting our fears to the faithfulness of God, our fear may be transformed into affirmation, and our denial to hope, as we proclaim *"this is the day that God has made, let us rejoice and be glad in it"* (Psalm 118:24, AP).

There is no antidote to mortality. But, process theology affirms that when there cannot be a cure, there can still be a healing. Healing at every stage of life is relational and theological. Process theology affirms the importance of positive visions of immortality in finding meaning in a world of change. Our actions do not perish but are immortalized in God's memory. Nothing is lost, everything of value is cherished by God as part of God's ongoing healing of the universe. Still, memory, even God's memory of our lives, may not be enough as stare into the abyss of mortality. While process theologians have a variety of visions of the afterlife from the finality of death to agnosticism and life within God's experience, I believe that the witness of near death, paranormal, and mystical experiences along with the biblical affirmation of Jesus' resurrection provides the foundation for affirming continuing spiritual and relational adventures beyond the grave. If God is omnipresent, intimate, and relational, then some of the most important values of this life will continue in the afterlife. As a tombstone in an historic cemetery affirms, "Dust to dust and ashes to ashes were never said of the soul." We will continue to evolve in a spiritual-relational environment, perhaps with few or no barriers between God and us and our creative alignment with God's vision for us. Everlasting life will not be isolating or unchanging but an ongoing living out of our particular gifts in the context of holy relatedness. While real and painful, death is not the end of our adventures but an open door into new possibilities. The hope for everlasting life enables us to face death while affirming the importance of our current lives.

For process theology, relationship is essential to facing life's unfixables. Healing relationships at life's descending edges of life require the willingness to listen, mirror, companion, and care for persons facing life-threatening illness. While there may not be a cure, there can be a healing, grounded in a sense of peace which goes beyond individual existence to join with world loyalty and the divine creativity. Holy relationships open us to our higher and larger selves. Our theology becomes embodied in imaginative reflection, loving touch, and faithful relatedness. The graceful interdependence of life, mediated through a caring community, invites to experience the providential relatedness of God. God's love, unconditional and all-encompassing, endures forever. "neither death, nor life, nor angels, nor rulers, nor things present, nor things to come, nor powers, nor height, nor depth, nor anything else in all creation, will be able to separate us from the love of God in Christ Jesus our Lord" (Romans 8:38–39).

CHAPTER SIX

WHERE ALL ARE PILGRIMS AND NONE ARE STRANGERS

Isaiah proclaims that God's house "shall be a house of prayer for all people" (Isaiah 56:7). This vision is embodied in my affirmation that the church's vocation is to be a community "where all are pilgrims and none are strangers." The calling of the church is to be a place where people can grow in wisdom and stature, align themselves with God's vision of Shalom, transform enemies into friends, and move from opposition to contrast.

Today, civility is in short supply, even in the church. Polarization characterizes our political lives, ethical thinking, and personal relationships. Politicians question the patriotism of persons who oppose their policies. Church leaders condemn as godless people with different values and lifestyles. Even people of similar political and theological viewpoints gracelessly critique one another for using yesterday's rather than the most current language to describe today's social, racial, and identity issues. Diversity has become a lightning rod for division instead of an opportunity for dialogue and enrichment. Psychologists and talk show hosts counsel people how to gather for holidays without disruptive disagreement!

Process theology recognizes that diversity can be a source of tension, but it also affirms the transformative power of differences. In art, religion, personal life, and politics, contrasting experiences often challenge our previous understandings of reality and awaken us to change. As an aesthetic and spiritual value, contrast and discord can invite us to growth, understanding, and change, and not defensiveness and denunciation. Once again, we need to remember the wisdom of one of my teachers Bernard Loomer, who asserted that spiritual stature involves:

> ...the range and depth of his love, his capacity for relationships... the volume of life you can take into your being and still maintain your integrity and individuality, the intensity and variety of outlook you can entertain in the unity of your being

36

without feeling defensive or insecure... the strength of your spirit to encourage others to become freer in the development of their diversity and uniqueness".[8]

Growth in stature is at the heart of the evolutionary process and each moment of experience. Process theology asserts that the universe aims at unity within diversity, and diversity within unity. Every actual occasion, the primary unit of reality, is an integration of the many factors — environment, past history, God's vision — in a unitive moment of experience. Higher organisms do not deny the diversity of reality — or eliminate discord — but initiate personal novelty to match the novelties of the environment, holding in contrast differing feelings and responses without negating their value in the process of creative transformation. We need to place some perspectives and feelings in the background to move forward or their great dissonance is debilitating, but even these must be included if we are to experience personal and spiritual growth. As uncomfortable as it may seem, Whitehead is correct in noting: "Progress is founded on the experience of discordant feelings. The social value of liberty lies in is production of discords. There are perfections beyond perfections. All realization is finite, and there is no perfection which is the infinitude of all perfections."[9]

One of the greatest pastoral care challenges of our time is nurturing creative contrast and diversity in personal relationships, congregational life, and the public sphere. As one commercial notes, "life comes at you fast" and the speed of change over the past fifty years has challenged social and religious norms that guided society for centuries. Technology has led to immediate contact with persons across the globe, the 24/7 news cycle, and an avalanche of information coming to us on a daily basis. Sadly, cultural and religious change has led to many persons hiding in siloes, listening to boutique new feeds that only reflect their opinions and life experiences, and seeing racial, sexual, religious, and political otherness as a mortal threat. The technology that was intended to join humankind as a single family, made up of diverse perspectives, has

8 Bernard Loomer, "S-I-Z-E is the Measure," Harry James Cargas and Bernard Lee, *Religious Experience and Process Theology* (Mahweh, NJ: Paulist Press, 1976), 70.
9 Alfred North Whitehead, *Adventures in Ideas,* 257.

led to greater isolation and antipathy. While cultural attitudes are changing in regards to diversity and pluralism in religion, sexuality, ethnicity, and lifestyle, these changes have created a cultural back-lash and a refusal to legitimize differing points of view.

Process theology is profoundly committed to a creative and centered pluralism in which our own comfort zones, personal perspective, and traditions are subject to review and transformation even as we honor — and maintain — what is important in our personal and communal identities. Process pastoral care seeks a creative synthesis, leading to honoring contrasting positions, through living in accordance with theological affirmations that enable us to grow in wisdom and stature:

The Universality of Revelation. Process theology believes, along with the Quakers, that there is something of God in everyone. God's presence is lively and contextual, and the quality of divine revelation is dependent in good measure on our openness to divine possibility within the welter of experience, including experiences of contrast and discordance. Still, like the rough-hewn geode, every life conceals something of beauty. The "holy otherness" of life challenges us to treat our neighbor with respect, regardless of her or his viewpoint or behavior. Even in the most challenging person, we meet, as Mother Teresa affirms, Christ in his distressing disguise.

Relativity of Perspective. Although divine revelation is universal, our experience of God — or any other significant reality — is always contextual. Our experiences are always shaped by our personal and cultural history, social, economic, and political location, and previous experience. We have our doctrinal and political "treasure in clay jars" (2 Corinthians 4:7). Our most cherished positions and perspectives beg for growth and transformation.

Constancy of process. The reality of process means that in order to be faithful to the truth, we must be constantly willing to revise our positions. There is no final resting place in our quest for quest. Every "absolute" is superseded by new "absolutes." Finality is an illusion in a world of process. As we look toward the far horizons of divine revelation, we are only given enough truth and wisdom for the next step. We must depend on divine illumination — and not the devices and desires of our hearts and intellect — for our salvation one step at a time.

Reality of limitation. The Apostle Paul recognized that "we see in a mirror dimly" and "know only in part" (1 Corinthians 13:12). Accordingly, in the spirit of theologian Reinhold Niebuhr's counsel, we must be aware of the truth in our neighbor's falsehood as well as the falsehood in our own truth. Humility is an essential theological, spiritual, relational, and political virtue. Our own limitations challenge us to look for truth wherever it is found and be willing to find common ground with persons of good faith whose beliefs and policies differ from our own, whether in congregational or political decision-making.

The Church as Sanctuary of the Spirit. The church of Christ as body of Christ is a sacred place and safe haven for humankind in its wondrous diversity. In a world where many suffer from anxiety, trauma, and fear, congregational safety is paramount. This involves not only "safe church" policies that protect children from predators, but also emotional and spiritual safety. Pastoral care necessitates that everyone who enters the church feel safe to express their viewpoint, share their feelings, reveal their doubts, and ask questions without fear of judgment or ostracism. The affirmation "you matter, your perspective is valuable, and your experience is important" is at the heart of process pastoral care. In spiritual sanctuary, we grow by faithful relatedness, even when revealed in contrasting experiences and perceptions. Today, this is especially important in responding to issues of sexuality, race, immigration, and politics, where often people are silenced by those who assume they have more power, privileged, or truth than their neighbors.

The quest for stature does not deny the difference between fact and opinion, truth and falsehood, or accuracy and inaccuracy, in our interpretations and responses. In open relationships, such appropriate judgments best occur in the context of respect, affirmation, listening, and safety. Even a misinterpretation or excessive emotional response to a particular situation can be the source of community and interpersonal growth, when we allow ourselves to be touched by another's life experiences. Once more, process theology roots empathetic pastoral care in our vision of God's tender care for each of us and God's willingness to adapt to our experience, looking for what can be saved even in difficult experiences and inviting us toward greater stature.

Ultimately, pastoral care from a process perspective involves the quest for beauty of experience — for everyone! Beauty involves embracing diversity, welcoming novelty, and affirming possibility. As a sanctuary for the production of beauty, the pastoral ministry of the church is a place of healing and incarnating God's vision on earth as it is in heaven.

BOOKS FOR THE JOURNEY

Cobb, John. *Theology and Pastoral Care*. Augsburg, 1967.

Coleman, Monica. *Bi-polar Faith: A Black Woman's Journey with Depression and Faith*. Fortress, 2016.

Coleman, Monica. *Not Alone: Reflections on Faith and Depression*. Inner Prizes, 2012.

Epperly, Bruce. *From Here to Eternity: Preparing for the Next Adventure*. Energion, 2016.

Epperly, Bruce. *Healing Worship: Purpose and Practice*. Pilgrim, 2006,

Epperly, Bruce. *Praying with Process Theology*. River Lane, 2017.

Epperly, Bruce. *Process Theology: A Guide for the Perplexed*. T&T Clark, 2011.

Epperly, Bruce. *Process Theology: Embracing Adventure with God*. Energion, 2014.

Epperly, Bruce. *Process and Ministry*. Energion, 2018.

Epperly, Bruce. *Process Spirituality: Practicing Holy Adventure*. Energion, 2017.

Epperly, Bruce. *Reiki Healing Touch and the Way of Jesus*. Northstone, 2005.

Epperly, Bruce. *The Energy of Love: Reiki and Christian Healing*. Energion, 2017.

Epperly, Bruce. *Healing Worship: Purpose and Practice*. Pilgrim, 2006,

Farmer, Patricia Adams. *Embracing a Beautiful God*. Create Space, 2013.

Jackson, Gordon. *Pastoral Care and Process Theology*. University Press of America, 1982.

Jackson, Gordon. *A Theology of Ministry: Creating Something of Beauty*. Chalice, 1998.

Nakashima, Rita and Brock and Rebecca Parker. *Proverbs from Ashes*. Beacon, 2002.

Nelson, Susan. *Healing the Broken Heart: Sin, Alienation, and the Gift of Grace*. Chalice, 1997.

TOPICAL LINE DRIVES

Straight to the Point in under 44 Pages

All Topical Line Drives volumes are priced at $5.99 print and $2.99 in all ebook formats.

Available

The Authorship of Hebrews: The Case for Paul	David Alan Black
What Protestants Need to Know about Roman Catholics	Robert LaRochelle
What Roman Catholics Need to Know about Protestants	Robert LaRochelle
Forgiveness: Finding Freedom from Your Past	Harvey Brown, Jr.
Process Theology: Embracing Adventure with God	Bruce Epperly
Holistic Spirituality: Life Transforming Wisdom from the Letter of James	
	Bruce Epperly
To Date or Not to Date: What the Bible Says about Pre-Marital Relationships	
	D. Kevin Brown
The Eucharist: Encounters with Jesus at the Table	Robert D. Cornwall
The Authority of Scripture in a Postmodern Age: Some Help from Karl Barth	
	Robert D. Cornwall
Rendering unto Caesar	Chris Surber
The Caregiver's Beatitudes	Robert Martin
What is Wrong with Social Justice	Elgin Hushbeck, Jr.
I'm Right and You're Wrong	Steve Kindle
Words of Woe: Alternative Lectionary Texts	Robert D. Cornwall
Stewardship: God's Way of Recreating the World	Steve Kindle
Those Footnotes in Your New Testament	Thomas W. Hudgins
Jonah: When God Changes	Bruce G. Epperly
Ruth & Esther: Women of Agency and Adventure	Bruce G. Epperly
Constructing Your Testimony	Doris Horton Murdoch
Christianity: The Basics	Elgin Hushbeck, Jr.
The Energy of Love	Bruce Epperly

(The titles of planned volumes may change before release.)

Generous Quantity Discounts Available
Dealer Inquiries Welcome
Energion Publications — P.O. Box 841
Gonzalez, FL 32560
Website: http://energionpubs.com
Phone: (850) 525-3916

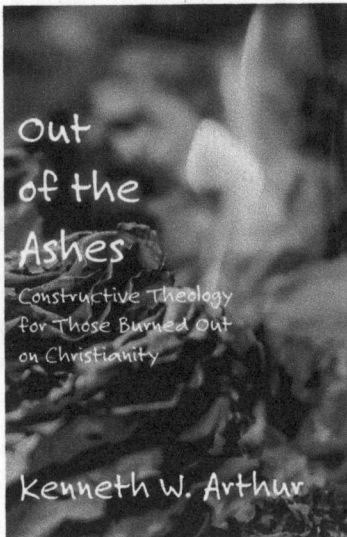

Out
of the
Ashes

Constructive Theology
for Those Burned Out
on Christianity

Kenneth W. Arthur

The book is theologically rich,
ministerially practical, and is
a unique contribution to the
continuing discussion regarding
progressive Christianity.

C. Drew Smith
Author of *Reframing a Relevant
Faith*

ALSO BY BRUCE EPPERLY

I asked Bruce Epperly for an in-
troduction to process theology in
12,000 words. I didn't think he
could do it.

He did.

Henry Neufeld, Publisher

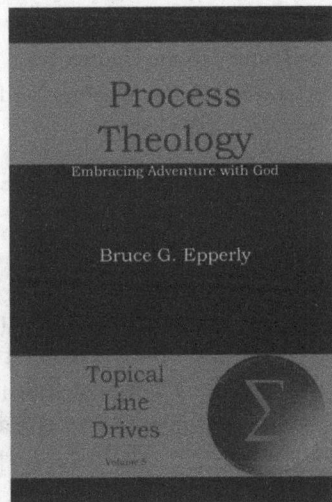

Process
Theology

Embracing Adventure with God

Bruce G. Epperly

Topical
Line
Drives

Σ

MORE FROM ENERGION PUBLICATIONS

Personal Study

Holy Smoke! Unholy Fire	Bob McKibben	$14.99
The Jesus Paradigm	David Alan Black	$17.99
When People Speak for God	Henry Neufeld	$17.99
The Sacred Journey	Chris Surber	$11.99

Christian Living

Faith in the Public Square	Robert D. Cornwall	$16.99
Grief: Finding the Candle of Light	Jody Neufeld	$8.99
Crossing the Street	Robert LaRochelle	$16.99
Life in the Spirit	J. Hamilton Weston	$12.99

Bible Study

Learning and Living Scripture	Lentz/Neufeld	$12.99
Inspiration: Hard Questions, Honest Answers	Alden Thompson	$29.99
Colossians & Philemon	Allan R. Bevere	$12.99
Ephesians: A Participatory Study Guide	Robert D. Cornwall	$9.99

Theology

Christian Archy	David Alan Black	$9.99
The Politics of Witness	Allan R. Bevere	$9.99
Ultimate Allegiance	Robert D. Cornwall	$9.99
From Here to Eternity	Bruce Epperly	$5.99
The Journey to the Undiscovered Country	William Powell Tuck	$9.99
Eschatology: A Participatory Study Guide	Edward W. H. Vick	$9.99
The Adventist's Dilemma	Edward W. H. Vick	$14.99

Ministry

Clergy Table Talk	Kent Ira Groff	$9.99
Thrive	Ruth Fletcher	$14.99
Out of the Office: A Theology of Ministry	Bob Cornwall	$9.99

Generous Quantity Discounts Available
Dealer Inquiries Welcome
Energion Publications — P.O. Box 841
Gonzalez, FL_ 32560
Website: http://energionpubs.com
Phone: (850) 525-3916

www.ingramcontent.com/pod-product-compliance
Lightning Source LLC
Chambersburg PA
CBHW011747020426
42331CB00014B/3315